Wednesday Afternoons with Dr. J

Written by Dr. Jonathan Jenkins, Psy.D

Illustrated by Lynn Jenner

This book is dedicated to all children who bravely enter therapy and talk about those difficult feelings.

A note to parents:

Thanks for stopping by my office; it is so nice to meet you. Before we start reading about Ari's adventures in psychotherapy, it is important that we have a discussion about your child's own potential experiences in therapy. For children, and for adults too, a doctor's office can be a scary place. This book was created to help orient children to some of the basics of psycho-therapy so that they can better adjust to the often-weird dynamic of talking about private thoughts or feelings with a stranger. This book is not only for children who are in need of mental health resources, but it is for all children so that they are more aware of psychology's inclusion in the healthcare system. Does anyone have any questions?

"So what is this story all about and who is Ari?"

Great question. This story was created as a therapeutic narrative, which means that it was created as a clinical tool to help children. As mentioned above, this book was created to help combat fears and misconceptions children might have about both psychologists and psychotherapy. This is done by exposing children to the story of Ari and his initial interactions with a therapist after experiencing the negative emotional impact of bullying. The story not only helps to explore with the reader what one can do in therapy, but it also sets the tone for the expectations of confidentiality and safety within the therapeutic space.

"What should we do after we read it to our child?"

After reading the story of Ari, I am sure that many children will still have a bunch of questions about therapy and that is great. If you feel comfortable having that conversation on your own, feel free to engage in an empowering conversation about therapy with your child and remind him or her that therapy is intended to be a safe place. If you feel uncomfortable, that is okay too. I recommend that you direct these questions to your child's clinician who could help co-facilitate that conversation before therapy starts or direct you to resources geared towards adults that further explain psychotherapy.

Well parents, thank you for stopping in but it is time for us to get to the fun part. I would like for everyone to meet Ari…

At 11:15 in the middle of May,
All of the children were at recess about to play,
But for little Ari something felt different today,
For little Ari something definitely felt a little different today.

That morning at breakfast he could barely eat,
And later in his favorite class he could barely sit in his seat,
For little Ari had something on his mind that he could not beat,
For little Ari had something on his mind that he definitely could not beat.

The thing on his mind was a secret sadness from inside,
A sadness that was so sad that he wanted it to go away and hide.
At first when it came he had paid it no mind,
But now it had grown and little happiness he could find,
But now it had grown and little happiness he could find.

Ari's parents then noticed this sadness and because they loved their son,
They hoped to return him to the days when he smiled and had fun.
They then searched day and night to find the one,
The one, the one to help their precious son.

And then in the middle of the night they came across a special name,
A person who was familiar with Ari's type of pain,
A psychologist who worked with children's feelings through play and game,

Oh what was that good ol' doctor's name?

"Dr. J?" Ari asked, "But who is he?
You know that going to the doctor is really scary for me.
Oh parents, this doctor I don't want to see,
I just know that he will give painful shots to me."

"Son, Dr. J. is a psychologist; he is unlike any doctor you've ever seen before,
Instead of giving you medicine to make you feel better, he will just want to
talk and maybe play some games on the floor.
But we can understand that you are probably scared or might think
it a horrible chore;
All we ask is that you bravely walk through that door."

After continuing to let his parents' comments about Dr. J. echo
through his mind,
On a Wednesday afternoon he noticed that it was his appointment time.
So with the love of his family in his heart and all of the bravery he could find,
Little Ari opened up the door to that psychologist's office and wondered
what inside he would find…

At the door he was greeted by this sort of tall guy with a funny looking tie and a noticeable twinkle in his eye.

"Good afternoon Ari, I'm excited to finally get the chance to say hi.

From what I've heard from your parents, you're one fun-loving little guy."

"I am a fun-loving guy Dr. J., I love games of all sorts:
I love board games, I love card games, I even love to play sports.
But lately I have not felt like doing any fun thing,
I'm scared, I'm sad, and I'm worried about what tomorrow might bring."

"Ari, openness like that is such a great tool.
I know that when you thought of telling other people about this you might
have felt silly or like a fool.
But that's not true young man, what you said is pretty cool,
Because nothing you ever say in here will be seen as stupid or silly.
This is my first rule."

"My second rule has to do with what is said in here.
I want you to be able to see this place as a space where you can
talk without fear.
What you say in here is private; it is only for my ear,
But if your safety were at risk that would be the only time something
you said would leave from here."

"And little Ari you're not alone! Feelings like these bother many girls and boys,
But in here, we will be curious about your feelings and explore them through
talk, make believe, and playing with toys.
So there's no need to be quiet in here! Feel free to be loud, feel free
to make noise!
Just know that we are proud of you for just coming in for our first meeting.
It took a lot of strength; it took a lot of poise."

"Dr. J, you certainly are unlike any doctor I've ever seen before,
You don't wear that funny long white coat like my other doctor wore.
I'm kind of nervous because this is different. It's an experience I've never had before,
So I think getting used to this may take awhile, it may take the next few appointments, maybe even more."

"And that's okay Ari, let me promise you that we are in no rush.
I can appreciate that talking about such things can be embarrassing,
difficult, or make you want to blush.
I just want you to not feel like you have to be quiet or hush,
Because communication seems to always help people turn some of the
scariest things in their lives into mush."

Ari nodded his head as he slowly began to feel more at ease.
He could then feel the nervous knot in his throat release him from its squeeze.
"Well, Dr. J., there are these older boys at school who like to tease.
They make fun of me so much that it makes me so sad and nervous,
it makes my mind and body freeze."

From that point on Ari and Dr. J. discussed this topic and what made his mind hurt so.

Week after week they met on Wednesday afternoons and tried to overcome these hurtful emotions, this terrible foe.

And as Ari grew more comfortable with his emotions, some he was able to better understand, some he was able to let go.

He started to slowly but surely return to that fun-loving guy that both his parents and he missed from long ago.

Each day in therapy was different; on many Wednesdays he came in excited, not knowing what to expect.

One day they acted with therapeutic puppets, the next week they worked on an emotions-related art project.

But all the while Ari knew from talking to Dr. J. what all these activities were for and what they were trying to inspect.

For it was Ari's emotions that Dr. J. wanted them to be curious about.

It was his sense of self and safety that he wanted to protect.

So as May turned into June and June turned into July,
Ari continued to spend his Wednesday afternoons with Dr. J., that sort of
tall kind of guy.

Emotions no longer seemed like something too scary to talk about, they were no longer something to defy.

For he had realized that everyone has good and bad emotions, they were something no one should be ashamed of or should deny.

So hooray for Ari, congratulations for being so brave!
You entered therapy without hesitation, like a daring knight entering a
dragon's deep dark cave.

And to you, young sir, a new road you are just beginning to pave,
Where you are more in control of your thoughts, feelings, and emotions
and no longer those things' slave.

About the Author

Dr. Jonathan Haywood Jenkins was born and raised in Natick, Massachusetts where he first fell in love with the Boston Celtics and cookie dough ice cream. After attending the University of Denver Graduate School of Professional Psychology where he specialized in pediatric neurodevelopment and multicultural psychology, he received further specialized clinical training at Cambridge Health Alliance/Harvard Medical School and at The Help Group where he was the Postdoctoral Fellow specializing in Autism Spectrum Disorders. Dr. Jenkins currently works at Massachusetts General Hospital both as a child and adolescent outpatient psychologist and as a member of the Harvard Medical School teaching community at the hospital. Dr. Jenkins also works as an outpatient psychologist in the Greater Boston community. When he is not working, he loves to create art, play sports, and spend time with his family.

About the Illustrator

Lynn Jenner is a professional illustrator and graphic designer living near Boulder, Colorado. When not busy illustrating and designing, she spends the rest of her free time running marathons and chasing after her two active young sons, two dogs and keeping up with her equally active husband.

www.ingramcontent.com/pod-product-compliance
Lightning Source LLC
Chambersburg PA
CBHW060811290526
45792CB00005BA/1604